JEN MUELLER

GAME
TIME

LEARN TO TALK SPORTS
IN 5 MINUTES A DAY

for Business

Game Time: Learn to Talk Sports in Five Minutes a Day *for Business*

Volume 1

Jen Mueller
Jen@TalkSportytoMe.com

Print Edition ISBN: 978-0-9893206-0-3
Kindle Edition ISBN: 978-0-9893206-1-0
EPUB Edition ISBN: 978-0-9893206-2-7

Cover design and interior text layout
by Kathryn E. Campbell, Gorham Printing
Printed in the United States of America.

Talk Sporty to Me
Bothell, WA
www.TalkSportytoMe.com

To the Jennifers; there's no one else like us.

Contents

CHAPTER 1

Why Become a Sports Fan?

YOU FEEL THE PRESSURE. You're sure everyone knows how to talk sports—except you. You notice it at work and when you're out with friends. The conversation turns to sports and you have nothing to say.

That changes today. This book will change your life and give you a practical, step-by-step strategy for becoming a fan and learning how to talk sports.

I turned a life-long love of sports and talking into a career as a sports broadcaster. Throughout my career, I have worked behind the scenes as a producer and have spent time in front of the camera as a sideline reporter and show host. I've worked closely with the Seattle Mariners, Seattle Seahawks, and a number of Northwest schools. In other words, I make my living talking sports.

There are a few things I know, as a result of my career. First, being able to talk sports opens doors. You'll understand how that works in the following paragraphs. Secondly, talking sports for business is very different from talking about a game at a tailgate or sports bar. If you're worried about having to learn all the rules and keeping track of stats, don't be. That's not the most effective way to talk about sports at work. Lastly, the most vocal sports fans you encounter don't have all the answers. Many of those fans believe that whoever has the last and loudest word wins, but that's not the case.

I can also tell you that if you feel left out, you're not alone.

I frequently hear from women and men who feel like they're on the outside looking in.

In fact, I founded my company, Talk Sporty to Me, after being approached by a group of female accountants in Seattle. They were smart and successful, but they had noticed a disturbing trend. Their male counterparts were inviting potential clients to sporting events like Mariners games.

At first, it simply looked like an expenditure of a few hours in the evenings, but over time these women realized the potential clients became clients and added tremendous value to their male counterparts.

A lack of sports knowledge or confidence in their sports knowledge was costing these women money. The women felt left out and didn't know where to start. About half the group considered themselves sports fans to some degree and the other half were starting from step one and needed to know the basics. That's how I initially developed this process of learning to talk sports in five minutes a day.

Women aren't the only ones who ask me for help.

There's a perception that men are born sports fans and that, from a young age, boys are drawn to athletics. My brother was one of those. He was the star quarterback and starting point guard in high school. He excelled at any sport he attempted and seemed to remember every stat he ever read.

Not everyone has that experience. I've met many men who spent their childhood pursuing other hobbies and didn't watch or play sports. Often those men will approach me at events when I'm away from the larger group and whisper the question, "Can you help me?"

When I ask them to elaborate, these men will say something like "I'm not a sports fan but it seems like everyone else is. I don't know how to talk sports and I don't know who to ask."

I have met these types of men from all walks of life: executives at software companies, sales professionals working with sports teams, students fresh out of college, and dads looking to connect with their kids.

I remember a conversation with one executive named Shawn who told me that most of the team he managed talked sports, and while he didn't fit into the conversations, he knew that as their manager he could come in and change the conversation and everyone else would follow.

The real problem arose when he and his wife would meet with other couples over dinner or at a party. The other men would stand around and talk about a recent game or sports story, the women would be talking amongst themselves, and he was caught in no-man's land, unable to join the conversation with the other men, but not wanting to upset the natural order of the group.

In Shawn's case, the personal outing felt more painful but the business implications are just as great.

Learning to talk sports for business is critical for:

- building rapport
- improving communication skills
- strengthening relationships
- increasing influence

It doesn't matter if you're male or female, sports conversations can influence your career and business opportunities.

It boils down to this—sports is part of our culture.

In the mid-2000s research done by the Pew Research Institute showed that 46 percent of Americans say they follow sports at least "somewhat." With the growing popularity of particular sports, like the National Football League, it's safe to round that number up to 50 percent. Stop and think about what this means for you. If you can talk sports and relate to sports fans you've got an "in" with about half the people in the United States.

The popularity of sports is one of the reasons sports metaphors are so popular in business and why so many comparisons are drawn between sports teams and business teams.

Simply ignoring the sports references and wishing they would go away is neither productive nor realistic. The numbers prove that sports fans are everywhere. Your best bet is to join in and use sports conversations to your advantage.

Take a look at why sports conversations give you an advantage at work.

Sports is DVR-proof. Gone are the days when everyone watches TV shows on the night they air. Digital video recorders enable viewers to watch shows on their time. Sports fans, however, will never watch TV this way. They will watch games, or at least highlights, within 24 hours of an event. This means there is fresh conversation material every day.

It's a foot in the door. If you want to do business with someone and identify that person as a sports fan, you can use a specific sporting event, like a big win, as an entry point into a bigger conversation.

Provides multiple follow-up opportunities. This is particularly important for sales teams that are trying to maintain relationships with clients. Sports seasons last for months, giving you something other than business to talk about every day during the season.

Increases influence. Sports fans talk to other sports fans. Job titles, income level, and status don't play a part in sports conversations. All fans have access to the same information and it evens the playing field in a conversation. Getting face time with key executives, decision-makers or influencers could be as easy as being able to connect with them on a favorite team or sport.

Improves productivity. Studies show that employees who feel valued give their best effort 93 percent of the time, compared with just 33 percent of employees who give their best effort when they don't feel valued at work. Talking about something other than work and something that a colleague is passionate about (like sports) helps you add value and increase productivity.

Allows you to stand out. The way you talk about games says a lot about you, and it enables you to judge the character of others. For example, do you complain about bad calls and a team getting shortchanged? Or are you a gracious loser and, more importantly, a gracious winner when talking about a game? If you have only a short amount of time to make a good impression, you've got to use every conversation to your advantage.

Increases your likability. When you appeal to large audiences and can meet them on their turf, you become more likeable, which increases the likelihood they will want to talk with you and do business with you.

Customizable. Sports conversations shouldn't be limited to just talking about the game. You can use sports conversations to talk about different parts of the country, particular players, or childhood memories, just to name a few ideas.

It's a "safe" subject. Unlike politics or religion, sports discussions are not likely to start a war of words in the break room. The goal in talking sports for business is to build rapport by talking more, not fighting more.

Small talk go-to. There's no need to engage in a two-hour conversation; simply making a quick comment about last night's game is enough to show an interest and keep the lines of communication open.

As we get started, keep in mind becoming a sports fan for business is more about gaining a working knowledge of sports news. Then having the ability to use the information effectively in a conversation without sounding awkward or feeling uncomfortable. The goal is build relationships and establish connections, both of which can happen without investing hours of your time watching games or highlights.

CHAPTER 2

Where Do I Start?

UP TO THIS POINT, if you type the question "How do I become a sports fan?" into any number of search engines, the general advice is "go to a game" or "watch a game"

Unfortunately that approach is about as helpful as asking "How do I learn how to cook?" and being dropped in the middle of a kitchen at the most popular restaurant in town. If that happened, the kitchen staff wouldn't explain the process of bringing water to a boil before adding pasta; they would just do it. Those instructions would be very helpful if you've never set foot in a kitchen to do more than make coffee or heat up a pizza.

That situation would be overwhelming and confusing.

Going to a game or watching a game if you're not a sports fan can feel the same way: overwhelming, confusing, and unproductive.

Here is the good news—becoming a fan doesn't have to be frustrating and you don't need to devote more than a few minutes a day to working on it.

I'm not going to promise that it won't feel uncomfortable at times. Just like a new cook has a tendency to keep looking back at a recipe to recheck the instructions, there may be a sense of "Am I doing this right?" I assure you there's no real right or wrong way to do it, as long as you're clear on your overall goal.

For example:

- Are you looking to join in the water-cooler conversations at work?
- Are you trying to solicit business from a specific company or client?
- Are you hoping to become more comfortable in social situations?

The overall goal is up to you, but here's why it's important: The sports world is extremely broad and can be very regionalized. For example, college football is popular in southern and southeastern states, while you'll find more professional football fans in the Northeast. Hockey fans are usually found in cold weather states, while baseball is more popular in warmer climates.

The following guidelines will help you determine where to focus your early efforts and how you can identify the teams and sports of interest to the people around you.

Choose from these categories and follow the specific suggestions to determine your starting point.

- Sport Specific
- Coworkers' Interests
- Regional Interest
- Personal Interests

The categories and suggestions are designed to eliminate the "shot in the dark" approach, or picking a starting point at random. Instead, this is a "best guess" plan that will help you make reasonable assumptions and be more effective.

Sport Specific Starting Point

Learning which sports rank among the most popular in the United States could provide some insight as to what most fans are following. The most popular sports were identified using Harris Poll surveys that asked fans to identify their favorite sport.

❶ If you want to start with the most popular sport, try the **NFL** (National Football League.) According to a 2012 Harris Poll, 59 percent of Americans follow the NFL. Its popularity has steadily grown over the last 15 years and shows no sign of decline.

❷ **Major League Baseball** (MLB) ranks a distant second to the NFL on the most popular sports in America lists. It is considered America's national pastime. Baseball's regular season lasts 162 games, which is the longest season of any sport. Compared with football, baseball is a slow sport with no time limit so the games can last from around two hours to more than three hours and longer.

❸ Professional basketball, in the form of the **NBA** (National Basketball Association), is the third most popular sport in America and its popularity is growing around the world. To meet the growing interest overseas, the 2012 NBA Finals were broadcast by 90 international media outlets.

❹ **College football** ranks fourth in popularity in the United States. College football fans are often drawn to the "amateur" status of the game as opposed to the NFL, where professionals can sign large contracts worth millions of dollars. College football is traditionally played on Saturdays, although in recent years more games take place on Thursday and Friday nights as well.

❺ The next most popular sports are somewhat dependent on the area of the country in which you live. (See the notes under using regional interests to choose a starting point.) In general, **college basketball** and the **NHL** (National Hockey League) are popular across the board.

Finding a Starting Point Based on Coworkers' Interests

One of the reasons you're learning to talk sports is to find common ground at work, so it makes sense that you might want to figure out which sport or team your coworkers want to talk about and start there.

1 Narrow the field by identifying a single coworker or client you'd like to talk to and pay attention to his or her surroundings. For example, does he or she have football memorabilia in the office? Does he or she wear a shirt on casual Fridays with a team or college logo on it? Or maybe the person has a Boston Red Sox license plate holder on the car? These are clues that can give you a starting point.

2 Each year many coworkers participate in **fantasy football,** which is one of the reasons it's grown to a $1 billion industry. Fantasy football is based on NFL players and teams. If you're in a workplace with a league, there's a good chance you're around NFL fans.

3 Similarly, each spring you'll likely see **March Madness brackets** circulating through the office. If so, you're around colleagues who follow college basketball, at least for the one-month stretch of the National Collegiate Athletic Association tournament. Because of the specific time frame of the NCAA tournament, it's a great time for you to jump in and commit to following college basketball during the tournament.

4 Golf is part of corporate culture especially at the executive level. If you work around sales and marketing teams, you might notice they participate in a handful of golf tournaments throughout the year. Often corporate golfers are interested in the PGA (Professional Golfers' Association) but that's not always the case. The focus here should be on your colleagues' experiences on the golf course first and then branch out and discuss the PGA storylines.

5 Do your colleagues participate in any **recreational sports leagues** through work? Use that information to drive the conversation and the learning curve. Here again, the focus is on your coworkers' experiences, not on the actual sport. For example, if there's a basketball team at work that plays a couple of days a week at lunch, ask about who had the best game or the best season.

Using Regional Interests to Choose a Starting Point

Each state or region can be identified by different tastes, weather, cultural habits, and sports. If you're taking a broad approach to sports, you could start by focusing on the teams and games that affect your region the most.

1 Recognize that **not all sports are of equal interest everywhere** in the country. For example, football tends to be bigger in the South while fans in the Northeast are more likely to follow college basketball or baseball.

2 To determine which sport takes top billing, take a look at the sports section of the local newspaper. The stories making the front page of the sports section, and specifically **the stories "above the fold,"** are of the most interest in your area.

3 Watching a local sportscast also provides information about the sports stories that are most pertinent to the region. The lead story or **the first story of the sportscast is the most importan**t. Another clue would be the overall amount of time dedicated to a particular sport, team, or athlete.

4 If you live or work in a city with **professional sports teams,** that's a good place to start. If there is more than one professional team in town, pay attention to how many jerseys or the amount of logoed apparel you see around town. Start with the team that has fans who appear more visible.

⑤ **Top college programs** can be as big for fans, if not bigger, than some professional teams. If you live a college town or near a college town, this could be a good starting point. As a general rule, focus on the football program and the men's basketball team as they typically have larger followings than other teams on campus.

Using Your Own Personal Interests as a Starting Point

Who says it always has to be about someone else? You can pick something that interests you and start your fandom there.

① Perhaps **you were an athlete** yourself. If so, there's a good chance you have better working knowledge of that sport than others or maybe you can relate to the challenges of the sport.

② Did you or your family have **a favorite team** growing up? Even if it's not relevant to the part of the country where you currently live, it's perfectly acceptable to cultivate your love of a specific team. The story behind your fandom is as interesting as the team itself.

③ Each sport offers a **different pace, time of game, and game flow.** Choose the one that appeals to you most. For example, baseball games aren't played with a time limit. Instead, each game is at least nine innings long, however long that takes. A football game, on the other hand, is a total of 60 minutes, but games typically last three hours because of the number of times the clock stops during the game. Soccer matches, on the other hand, are 90 minutes long. The clock runs during the entire match, so you can expect to spend about two hours watching a soccer game, allowing for a 20-minute halftime.

❹ Sometimes finding a starting point is as easy as **identifying a favorite player**. A favorite player could be the most inspiring player you've seen, the hardest working, the best player in a sport, or perhaps the best looking player on a team. Whatever the reason you identify with him or her, use that as motivation to check in on that player on a regular basis. You might be focused on a singular player at first, but along the way, you'll also be learning more about a team and sport.

❺ **The sport your kids play or watch** offers another starting point. No one said you have to follow professional sports to be a fan. Grow your knowledge with your kids, either as they advance in their careers or as they themselves watch more sports. Take time to watch together as a family and watch your fandom grow.

Once again, there's no right or wrong way to go about becoming a fan. It's far more important to just get started and be consistent with growing your knowledge base.

CHAPTER 3

Five Steps in Five Minutes

THINK BACK to the cooking example in the beginning of Chapter 2. When you're trying to achieve a certain outcome in the kitchen, a recipe comes in handy. It's a step-by-step guide that gets you from start to finish.

We are going to use a similar process to build a sports knowledge base.

Jumping into all the current sports headlines can feel a bit like trying to drink from a fire hydrant. There's an endless amount of information available and making sense of it all is impossible.

The following five-step process is an organized and efficient way to increase your knowledge base, stay current on hot sports topics, and make sure you don't overextend yourself in trying to do too much too soon.

Ideally this process will become part of your daily routine and in a matter of weeks you'll be much more at ease when the conversation turns to sports.

Step 1 Read sports headlines

This really is as straightforward as it sounds. The headlines on the front page of the sports section in your local newspaper provide much more information than you realize.

Here's an example of a headline from *The Seattle Times* on June 8, 2012.

- "Mariners no-hit the Dodgers with 6 Different Pitchers. Kevin Millwood gets no-hitter rolling."

Take a look at how much information that headline provides:

❶ We know which teams were playing the Mariners and Dodgers

❷ We know what happened—the Mariners didn't allow a hit to the Dodgers

❸ We know who was involved—6 different pitchers

❹ We know how it started—Kevin Millwood gets no-hitter rolling

❺ The accompanying picture showed players on a baseball field, indicating the sport referred to in the headline was baseball.

That's a total of five pieces of information just on the surface of that headline. These bullet points become your nuggets of information to interject in conversations. The key is to be nonchalant. Don't try too hard. Let the conversation unfold naturally.

Here's how that information might look in a conversation if a sports-loving coworker approached you before meeting and asked you about the game. Notice your potential responses based strictly on the information in the headline.

How about that Mariners game last night?

Yeah, a no-hitter against the Dodgers.

> **Kevin Millwood was awesome; too bad he got hurt and had to come out of the game. Good thing the M's bullpen finished the job.**

> **It took six pitchers to get it done.**

> **That doesn't happen often; it was a great win.**

You'll notice in this conversation that the sports-loving coworker provided even more information than was given in the headline. That's a benefit to you because now you have even more tidbits to use in future conversations. Don't worry about learning every detail of the game. It's not necessary. Sports fans will pick up the conversation and run with it.

One more note about reading the local sports headlines: when possible, I do recommend you read them from the actual sports page itself versus going online. (We'll get to how to approach online content next.) The sports page helps you decipher the most important information quicker, and provides more information than a website. Anything in bold type on a sports page is considered a headline for our purposes, which includes the main headlines, subheadlines, and the captions under pictures. You have to navigate through a few pages on many newspaper websites to get the same layout and information.

Step 2 Log on to one sports-related website

There are literally hundreds you can choose from but make it easy on yourself and check one or two of the big ones like ESPN.com or the site I prefer, CBSSports.com. When you log on to either of those sites, you'll notice a set of headlines on the right side of the screen. The reason I prefer CBSSports.com is because the first sentence pops up on many of the stories when you move your cursor over the headline. It's just like reading a second headline without double clicking and waiting for the story to load.

The difference between reading the headlines in a newspaper and going online is perspective. If you're reading a local newspaper, you're getting information that is pertinent to the readership in that specific area. As a note, if you're traveling you should read the headlines in the city you're visiting to gain the perspective of the locals.

Websites like ESPN.com and CBSSports.com give the national perspective. They cover the biggest stories making news around the country and provide a mix of all sports and storylines.

The information you glean from those headlines might not be useful right away but will help you to build a broader knowledge base. In fact, it's entirely possible to follow a major story without ever reading a story.

The following headlines from ESPN.com give a pretty good outline of the Tiger Woods saga that derailed his career for two years.

- Tiger Woods injured in early-morning car crash
  (ESPN.com November 20, 2009)

- Tiger Woods issues Web statement: "I am far short of perfect"
  (ESPN.com December 3, 2009)

- Tiger Woods taking "indefinite break" from golf amid scandal
  (ESPN.com December 12, 2009)

- Tiger Woods at Mississippi sex rehab clinic
  (ESPN.com January 20, 2010)

- Tiger Woods, Elin Nordegren officially divorce
  (ESPN.com August 23, 2010)

- Tiger Woods ends two-year drought with win at Chevron
  (December 5, 2011)

- Tiger Woods wins at Bay Hill, ends PGA tour slump
  (March 25, 2012)

Here is an example of how you could use this information knowledge base in a conversation following a recent Tiger win. In this example, a colleage is striking up a conversation and you are responding.

> **Tiger Woods won over the weekend.**

> **Looks like he's back on track.**

> **He's hitting the ball well and seems to have solved the problems in his short game. He's on track to win a lot more.**

> **That's a change. He didn't get a win for two years. Guess everything is in the past now.**

Notice that you don't need to go into a lot of detail in the exchange. You can use common sense to piece together the overall theme, and allow a sports-loving colleague to fill in the gaps.

Step 3 Listen to a daily radio update

This step allows you to multitask during your drive to and from work. If you're listening to a local radio station, you'll hear traffic and weather reports combined with news headlines. Many times there's a sports note buried in those headlines. It's short, sweet, and to the point, which is perfect for your busy schedule.

A typical radio update will sound like this:

> "Miami beat Oklahoma City in Game 2 of the NBA Finals. The series is tied at a game apiece. Game 3 is tomorrow night."

Here's another example:

> "The Mariners complete the sweep of the Twins. The M's start a three-game series tonight against the Texas Rangers."

The information in a radio update is typically more basic than the information you'll find in a headline or online, but don't discount its value. Simply knowing that there's a game in town or understanding that most fans will be tuned in to a big game gives you chance to fit in and be part of the conversation.

Here's an example of how you can use this information in a conversation:

The Miami–Oklahoma City series is a good one.

It's even at a game apiece, right?

> **Yeah, and I can't wait to see how LeBron James and Kevin Durant respond. They're shooting really well right now.**

> **Next game is tomorrow, right?**

> **Yep, and I'll be watching for sure.**

Notice the exchange is almost as brief as the update itself. All of our conversation examples are short because that's the way many of the conversations play out in real life. You don't need to carry on a 20-minute conversation about a game or a player. That information you're gathering in this process is designed to help you break the ice and begin building rapport and relationships.

Step 4 Watch Ticker Lines

The ticker line is the information that scrolls at the bottom of the screen. You see it quite often on news channels like CNN or MSNBC, which provide up-to-the-minute information on the stock market, breaking news, and daily updates. You'll also see ticker lines quite a bit on morning shows where the information includes rush hour drive time, traffic, and weather reports.

In the sports world, no one utilizes a ticker better than ESPN. If you've ever watched a game or caught a few minutes of SportsCenter—even if it's because someone else turned to that channel—you'll notice the lines of information at the bottom of the screen. That information could be anything from game statistics, scores or headlines, the very same headlines that you might find online or in a newspaper. The upside to watching the ticker line in addition to Steps 1-3 is the immediacy with which you get the latest news.

Here is an example of what a ticker line might say:

- **Breaking News:** The Red Sox fire Terry Francona following late-season collapse. The Red Sox lost 20 of 27 games in September.

Using the information in a conversation can work the same way as described in steps 1-3, but in this next conversation example you'll see a new twist you can use after a coworker comments on the breaking news.

> **I can't believe the Red Sox fired Francona.**

> **I saw that yesterday on SportsCenter.**

> **I wonder who they'll get to replace him.**

> **I don't know, but after that September collapse they'll have a lot of work to do.**

Did you see the new wrinkle in this conversation? You not only added information to the conversation but you casually mentioned that you discovered it while watching SportsCenter. This does two things. First, it helps establish your credibility and second, it shows that you are interested in sports enough to watch SportsCenter. You'll also notice in the final comment "you" made that "you" were honest when you said you didn't know who would be the next manager and then you added your tidbit of information. It's important to note that honesty is the best policy. Your parents and teachers told you that and I'm going to reiterate it here. Don't try to lie your way through a conversation.

Step 5 Participate in a sports-related conversation

By this point in the process, you've seen four examples of how to engage in a sports conversation. You've learned how to take what appears to be very basic information and turn it into a quick, useful exchange. This step is on the list as a reminder that your goal should be to participate in at least one sports-related conversation a day, because without practice it never gets easier.

Your participation could come in a few ways. You can be an active listener, a willing respondent, or the conversation driver.

Each of the previous conversation examples put you in the role of willing respondent so you're familiar with how that looks. If you're playing the role of active listener, you are conveying your interest and participation through body language. In that case, you might be part of a large group of coworkers who are engaged in a discussion about a particular game from last weekend. Instead of jumping into the fray, you watch it play out and nod appropriately to show you're listening and, at the same time, taking mental notes about the subject matter. Remember one piece of information from that conversation can be just as helpful as Steps 1-4.

Being a conversation driver means you're the one who starts the discussion. You'll need to grow comfortable with this aspect of sports conversations because at some a point you will need to start the conversation and break the ice.

Here's a general example of how you might spark a conversation:

> **Did you watch any of the game yesterday?**

> **I only watched about half. It was about what I expected, not much scoring.**

> **You watched more than me; I only watched for a few minutes. I had a lot going on between my travel schedule and our meeting this week.**

> **I know what you mean. I feel like there's not enough time to get it all done.**

This is a very different type of conversation than in the previous examples but it does a couple of different things. One, it establishes you as the person controlling the conversation, and that means you can steer it however you choose. Two, it shows that a "sports conversation" doesn't have to strictly be about sports. This example starts by asking about last night's game and then transitions to the heavy work schedule. This is a great use of a sports conversation because it helped to break the ice and lead you into work talk.

You might be wondering why the five-step process doesn't mention apps or social media. Those are certainly ways to access information, but it's harder to control the amount of information. You don't need to learn everything all at once. Take it at your own pace, and add on when you're ready.

One final note about using this five-step process; it's designed to give you bullet points and headlines, not every detail of every story. Don't worry about what you don't know; focus on the information you do have. I promise that it's more than enough to have a conversation with a savvy sports fan.

The goal should be to complete all five steps every day, but any combination of them will get the job done.

CHAPTER 4

Reading Box Scores and Street Cred Tips

THE NEXT FEW PAGES contain helpful information regarding basic sports facts. You'll see examples of box scores, which provide more detail that just the final score. In fact, it's possible to tell the story of a game simply by reading the box score. You'll see examples of that for each sport.

In addition, you'll also find a quick rundown of how points are scored in each of the major sports and a "street cred" tip that will help establish your credibility and make you sound like a sports fan.

Reading the Box Scores:

General notes about box scores:

- The home team is listed across the bottom of the box score and the visiting team is listed across the top.

- The numbers next to each team name indicate the team's overall record and are listed as within brackets as (wins–losses).

- If people are talking about the "offense" in a game, they're referring to the points scored.

- Defense refers to a team's ability to prevent the opponent from scoring.

Street Cred Tip #1: When saying a score in conversation, give the winning team score first.

Incorrect: "The Mets lost 3 to 9."

Correct: "The Mets lost 9-3."

Incorrect: "The Miami Heat lost 87–95 to Oklahoma City."

Correct: "The Heat lost 95–87. Or Oklahoma City beat Miami 95–87."

Street Cred Tip #2: Most sports fans refer to athletes by their last names only. So don't worry about remembering all the first names. There are a few exceptions like Tiger Woods and LeBron James and, in that case, you can use either first, last, or both names.

How points are scored

Football:

Touchdowns = 6 points

Extra point = 1 point

Field Goal = 3 points

2-point conversion = 2 points

Safety = 2 points

Basketball:

3-point shots = 3 points

Free Throw = 1 point

Field Goal = 2 points

*Field goals are any shot other than 3 pointer or free throw

Baseball:

Runs = 1 point

Hockey:

Goals = 1 point

Soccer:

Goals = 1 point

Let's Talk About it: Baseball Box Score

	1	2	3	4	5	6	7	8	9	R	H	E
Chi Cubs	0	0	1	1	1	0	3	0	3	9	14	0
NY Mets	0	1	0	0	0	0	0	2	0	3	6	1
W: Silva, C (2–0) L: Perez, O (0–2)												

You'll notice the numbers across the top denote the innings of the game. So it's easy to read the line and see at what point in the game each team scored. The final score is listed under the column marked "R." The column marked "H" is the total hits by each team and the "E" column is for errors committed during the game.

The home team is across the bottom (NY Mets) and the visiting team (Chi Cubs) is across the top. In baseball the visiting team bats first followed by the home team.

The additional information in the last row indicates the winning pitcher was C. Silva (written in a box score as: Silva, C.) The numbers after his name indicate his win-loss record. In this case Silva has won two games and hasn't lost a game. The losing pitcher was O. Perez. His record is zero wins and two losses.

This box score tells the entire story of the game, even if you didn't see a single highlight.

Here's an example of how the story could be told.

- "The Mets scored first, but the Cubs came right back and scored in three straight innings, before breaking open the game with three runs in the seventh. The Mets rallied with a couple runs in the eighth but the Cubs pounded out 14 hits and won 9–3."

It could also be as simple as saying:

- "The Cubs were all over the Mets. Chicago blew 'em out 9–3."

Street Cred Tip #1: Don't refer to the score in "points." **Baseball is scored in runs.**

Incorrect: "The Mets lost by 6 points."

Correct: "The Mets lost by 6 runs."

Street Cred Tip #2: If a game is tied after nine innings, the teams play extra innings, not overtime.

Incorrect: "If this game stays tied they're going to have to play overtime."

Correct: "If this game stayed tied they're going into extra innings."

Let's Talk About It: NBA Basketball Box Score

Final	1	2	3	4	T
New York (48–26)	23	24	21	27	**95**
Atlanta (42–34)	18	22	28	14	**82**
Players of the Game NY—Carmelo Anthony (Pts: 40, Reb: 5, Ast: 3) ATL—Kyle Korver (Pts: 25, Reb: 6, Ast: 4)					

The numbers across the top of these scores indicate the four quarters of a basketball game. In some scores you'll notice the box labeled "OT." That stands for overtime and it happens when the score is tied at the end of four quarters. There is a break after the first two quarters for halftime.

The numbers following each of the teams indicate the overall record for the team. Remember wins are listed first followed by the losses. In this example New York has won 48 games and lost 26 games.

The section of the box marked "players of the game" lists the players who contributed the most in the game. In the game between New York and Atlanta, you can tell that Carmelo Anthony scored 40 points, had five rebounds and three assists.

Here's an example of how to tell the story of the game without watching it.

- "New York took the early lead against Atlanta. They closed it out with a strong fourth quarter. Carmelo Anthony scored 40 points to help New York win 95–82."

Look at the score in the San Antonio/Toronto game.

Final	1	2	3	4	T
San Antonio (44–8)	31	29	21	30	**111**
Toronto (14–39)	29	27	28	16	**100**
Players of the Game SA—DeJuan Blair (Pts: 28, Reb: 11, Ast: 0) TOR—DeMar DeRozen (Pts: 25, Reb: 4, Ast: 4)					

Here's an example of a more general game description that would work well in a conversation:

- "Did you see the offense in Toronto? Both teams hit the century mark. It was San Antonio coming out on top though."

Street Cred Tip: The term "century mark" refers to hitting 100 points in a game. When talking about this accomplishment, you can say century mark or comment that both teams hit "a hundred," not "one hundred" points.

Incorrect: "Did you see Toronto scored 100 points and San Antonio scored 111 points?"

Correct: "San Antonio beat Toronto one-eleven to 100."

Let's Talk About It:
College Basketball Box Score

Final	1	2	T
Wisconsin #22 (23–11)	24	19	43
Ohio State #10 (26–7)	23	27	50
Players of the Game OSU—Deshaun Thomas (Pts: 17, Reb: 7, Ast: 1) WISC—Traevon Jackson (Pts: 10, Reb: 3, Ast: 2)			

A box score from a college basketball game is a little different from an NBA box score. The numbers across the top of the score indicate two halves instead of four quarters like in the previous example. Each half is 20 minutes long with a break, or halftime, between the first and second half.

Next to the school names you see a number followed by the team record. This indicates the national ranking of the team. In this box score Wisconsin is ranked as the 22nd best team in the country and Ohio State is the 10th best team. The win-loss records are in parentheses. In this example Wisconsin has won 23 games and lost 11. Ohio State has won 26 games and lost seven.

Just like in the NBA box score, the players of the game section lists the top two contributors in the game.

Here's an example of how you could talk about this game based solely on the box score:

- "It was a close first half between Wisconsin and Ohio State. But Ohio State turned it up in the second half to avoid an upset. Deshaun Thomas scored 17 points helping Ohio State win 50–43."

Street Cred Tip: First-year players in college are called freshmen. In professional sports, first-year players are called rookies.

Incorrect: "Did you see how well that rookie played for Michigan?"

Correct: "Did you see how well that freshman played for Michigan?"

Let's Talk About It: **Football Box Score**

Cowboys Stadium (Arlington, TX)						
Final		1	2	3	4	T
Pittsburgh (14–5–0)		0	10	7	8	25
Green Bay (14–6–0)		14	7	0	10	31

Game Leaders: Steelers	**Packers**
Pass: B. Roethlisberger (25–40, 263)	A. Rodgers (24–39, 304)
Rush: R. Mendenhall (14–63)	J. Starks (11–52)
Rec: M. Wallace (9–89)	J. Nelson (9–140)

There's a lot of information in a football box score. Gathering all the pieces sometimes requires a little math. That's because you can't score one point at a time; there has to be something else that preceded that one point. Refer back to the box "How they score" for the point totals.

This box score is set up like the others we've seen. The four boxes along the top denote the quarters and the "T" gives the total score. There is a break after the first two quarters for halftime.

The game leaders section lists the best performers of the day. Football fans are concerned with three key areas of offense: passing (throwing the ball), rushing (running the ball), and receiving (catching the ball).

In this box score you can see that B. Roethlisberger led the Steelers in passing. The numbers following his name list the number of completed passes, the total number of passes attempted, and the total yards of those passes. In football, you can attempt a pass without it being caught, which is why the number of completed passes is noted.

In Roethlisberger's case he completed 25 passes and attempted 40 throws. The completed passes equaled 263 yards.

It's easier when looking at the rest of the stats listed. Let's look at J. Starks in the "Rush" category. The first number indicates the number of times he rushed, or ran the ball. The second number tells you the total number of yards he gained. In Starks' case he carried the ball 11 times and ran for a total of 52 yards.

Finally, let's look at the receivers. It's similar to the rushing statistic. The first number tells you the number of passes he caught and the second tells you the total yards of those catches. So J. Nelson caught nine passes for a total of 140 yards.

Just like the other scores we've looked at, you can tell the story of the game by reading the box score, but it's a little different because teams typically score in increments of seven or three. A touchdown is worth six points but most teams make the extra point attempt that follows, which is why we tend to think of touchdowns equaling seven points. It's also how you can tell Green Bay scored two touchdowns in the first quarter. In the second quarter, Pittsburgh scored a touchdown and kicked a field goal because seven plus three equals 10. So what happened in the fourth quarter? Pittsburgh scored a touchdown and decided to go for a two-point conversion following the TD instead of the extra point. That's how the team earned eight points instead of seven on the touchdown.

Here's an example of how you could talk about this game without watching it:

- "Green Bay jumped out to an early lead, scoring two touchdowns in the first quarter. Pittsburgh put 10 points on the board before halftime but Green Bay still held a lead. Pittsburgh added a TD in the third but Green Bay held on to win 31–25."

Street Cred Tip: Don't use the word "points" to describe the final score of a game. Simply give the score.

Incorrect: "Green Bay won by six points."

Correct: "Green Bay won 31–25."

It is also acceptable to note how many touchdowns or field goals a team won by. For example:

"Seattle beat Arizona by a touchdown, 21–14."

Or "Chicago beat Green Bay by a field goal, 17–14."

Let's Talk About it: Hockey Box Score

Final SO	1	2	3	OT	SO	T
Tampa Bay (28–15–5)	1	0	1	0	1(2)	**3**
Atlanta (23–18–8)	1	1	0	0	0(1)	**2**
Three Stars S. Stamkos—TB (Goals: 2, Assists: 0) D. Moore—TB (Goals: 0, Assists: 0) N. Bergfors—ATL (Goals: 1, Assists: 0)						

Hockey scores are a little different than the previous box scores you've seen.

The numbers across the top note the three periods of a game. There is no halftime during the game. In hockey they have two intermissions, one after the first period and the other after the second period. You'll also see in the Tampa Bay/Atlanta game boxes labeled "OT" and "SO." "OT" stands for "overtime" and "SO" stands for "shootout."

In hockey, a game that is tied after three periods goes into overtime. If it's still tied after that, the game goes to a shootout. The winner of the shootout wins the game. So in the case of the Tampa Bay/Atlanta game, Tampa Bay won the shootout two goals to one as you see by the numbers in parenthesis.

Hockey games can end in a tie, which is why there are three numbers next to each team name. That is the overall team record. The first number gives the wins, the second gives the losses, and third is the number of tie games each team has played.

The last row lists three players who contributed the most in the game. The name is given as first initial followed by last name. Then you'll see a team abbreviation, in this case TB stands for Tampa Bay. That is followed by their stats. In this example Tampa Bay's S. Stamkos scored 2 goals.

Here's an example of how you would talk about that game in a conversation:

- "Atlanta was up 2–1 heading into the third period but Tampa Bay scored to force overtime. The game went to a shootout and Tampa won the shootout 2–1. They won the game 3–2."

Here's another example:

Final	1	2	3	T
Ottawa (17–24–7)	0	2	0	2
Philadelphia (31–11–5)	2	1	3	6
Three Stars: M. Richards—PHI (Goals: 2, Assists: 2) D. Briere—PHI (Goals: 1, Assists: 1) A. Meszaros —PHI (Goals: 1, Assists: 1)				

- "Philadelphia was on fire. They scored in every period and ended up winning 6–2."

Street Cred Tip #1: If you see a score of "0" in a hockey game, don't use the word "zero" when giving the score of the game.

Incorrect: "New Jersey won two to zero."

Correct: "New Jersey won two-zip" or "New Jersey blanked Pittsburgh two-nothing."

Street Cred Tip #2: Don't refer to the final score as points. Hockey is scored in goals.

Incorrect: "Carolina beat New York by three points."

Correct: "Carolina beat New York by three goals."

Let's Talk About It: Golf Leaderboard

Pos	Player Name	Today	Thru	To Par	R1	R2	R3	R4	Total Score
1	Webb Simpson	-2	F	+1	72	73	68	68	281
T2	Graeme McDowell	+3	F	+2	69	72	68	73	282
T2	Michael Thompson	-3	F	+2	66	75	74	67	282
T4	Jason Dufner	E	F	+3	72	71	70	70	283
T4	Jim Furyk	+4	F	+3	70	69	70	74	283
T4	Padraig Harrington	-2	F	+3	74	70	71	68	283
T4	John Peterson	E	F	+3	71	70	72	70	283
T4	David Toms	-2	F	+3	69	70	76	68	283
9	Ernie Els	+2	F	+4	75	69	68	72	284

Golf's version of a box score is called the leaderboard. (See notes on Golf Terms)

Let's look across the leaderboard and decipher the boxes. "Today" indicates where the golfer is in relation to "par" during the round. A minus sign indicates he is under par, which is good. And a plus sign indicates he is over par, which is bad. "Thru" indicates which hole on the course he or she has completed. In this case, every golfer is finished because this is the final leaderboard standings from a U.S. Open. "To Par" tells you the golfers' relation to par for the entire tournament. R1–R4 gives the individual scores for each round of golf played during the four-day tournament. The "Total Score" is just that, the total number of strokes it took each golfer to complete the tournament. The lower the score the better the golfer fared.

You'll notice on the left side of the player's name there is a "pos" listing. That's the order the players finished. Players can tie for any position outside of the overall champion. Thus the T2, T4, etc…

If you were to talk about this golf tournament without watching, you could say something like this:

- "Webb Simpson turned in a solid final two rounds while Graeme McDowell struggled during the final round. He was three over par and missed his chance at the win. Simpson won by one stroke."

Street Cred Tip #1: Don't use points when describing golf scores. Golf is scored by strokes.

Incorrect: "Simpson beat McDowell by a point."

Correct: "Simpson beat McDowell by one stroke."

Street Cred Tip #2: Unless the tournament is over, don't ask about who's "winning" the tournament. Ask about who's at the top of the leaderboard.

Incorrect: "Is Ernie Els winning after three rounds?"

Correct: "Who's leading after three rounds?" Or "Who's at the top of the leaderboard?"

Golf terms:

Par – Strokes it should take to complete the hole

Birdie – One stroke under par

Eagle – Two strokes under par

Bogey – One stroke over par

Double Bogey – Two strokes over par

 **Let's Talk About It: Soccer Box Score**

FT	Toronto FC	2-2	Los Angeles
16′		0-1	Mike Magee
29′	Robert Earnshaw	1-1	
78′	Jonathan Osorio	2-1	
90′+2′		2-2	Jose Villarreal

In comparison to the rest of the box scores, there isn't as much going on here.

In this soccer box score, the teams and the final score are listed across the top. The match was played between Toronto FC and Los Angeles and ended in a 2–2 tie. "FC" is short for football club, which is what it's called in many countries. That's why sometimes you'll hear people making the distinction between American football (think college football and the NFL) and soccer. The abbreviation "FT" stands for Final Time, which is another way of saying the game is final or over.

You'll see no periods or quarters like in the other box scores. That's because soccer is a timed sport. The games are 90 minutes long with a halftime break at the 45-minute mark. The clock starts at 00:00 and counts up to 90.

When you look at the score, you see a column under "FT" marking time. That's the time in the game when the goal was scored. Mike Magee scored in the 16th minute to give Los Angeles the lead.

Notice the 90′ + 2′ on the last line. That means the goal was scored in "stoppage time." After 90 minutes, the referee on the field determines how much extra time should be played based on any stoppages during the game. Those stoppages might happen during an injury or a discussion with a ref.

A quick recap of this game in conversation could sound like this:

- "Los Angeles took the early lead, but Toronto answered with a pair of goals. Toronto led 2–1 after 90 minutes, but Jose Villarreal scored in stoppage time. What an exciting finish for LA! The game ended in a 2–2 draw."

Street Cred Tip #1: Soccer teams play "matches," not games.

Incorrect: "Vancouver won the game against Colorado."

Correct: "Vancouver won the match against Colorado."

Street Cred Tip #2: A score of "0" is stated as "nil."

Incorrect: "Vancouver won 1–nothing."

Correct: "Vancouver won 1–nil."

Street Cred Tip #3: Soccer is played on a pitch, not a field.

Incorrect: "The players are getting ready to hit the field."

Correct: "The players are getting ready to take the pitch."

CHAPTER 5

Sports Season Reference Guide

NOW THAT YOU KNOW how to build your sports knowledge base and read a box score, it's time to take a closer look at sports seasons. While it might feel like football is all your coworkers ever talk about, football games are only played from August through January. It might seem like baseball season lasts all year, yet games are played from March through October.

Arming yourself with information about when sports seasons start and stop gives you the best chance of choosing a relevant conversation topic.

The chart details the general timeline for each sports season and narrows down key months for tennis and horse racing.

Sports Seasons Reference Guide

	Jan	Feb	March	April	May	June	July	Aug	Sept	Oct	Nov	Dec
Pro Football												
College Football												
Football Bowls												
Pro Basketball												
College Basketball												
Baseball												
Hockey												
Golf												
Soccer												
Auto Racing												
Horse Racing												
Tennis												

When it comes to horse racing and tennis, many events occur throughout the entire year. The months selected on the chart indicate key events in both sports.

The Triple Crown races in horse racing are the most important events of the year. The races are the Kentucky Derby, the Preakness Stakes, and the Belmont Stakes. They take place in May and June every year. The Triple Crown refers to the achievement of winning all three races in a single calendar year.

Tennis has a similar set of events that make up the Grand Slam. Those tournaments are the Australian Open, French Open, Wimbledon, and U.S. Open. To win the Grand Slam title, a player must win all four major championships in a single calendar year.

Golf also has a set of Major Championships. These four events are more prestigious than other tournaments throughout the year: the Masters, the U.S. Open, the British Open, and the PGA Championship. Key months for those events are April, June, July, and August, respectively.

You'll notice the chart does not account for non-annual events like the Winter Olympics, Summer Olympics, or World Cup. Those events are held every four years at various sites. You'll know when it's time to start talking about and paying attention to those events based on the amount of media coverage and fan excitement.

In Chapter 4 we identified ways to talk about sporting events based on box scores regardless of whether you had watched the game. You can use a similar approach using the information in the chart to strike up a conversation. Here are a few examples:

> **Football season is right around the corner. Are you a fan?**

> **With basketball coming up, who do you think has the best team this year?**

> **I know you're a baseball fan; how's your team looking this year?**

There's one more note relating to sports conversations and your colleagues. Make sure you know your audience. Asking a hockey fan about an upcoming golf tournament or asking a baseball fan about the start of football season probably won't resonate and likely won't spark much of a conversation.

You can refer back to Chapter 2 for ideas on how to figure out which sports interest your colleagues, or simply ask the question as in the previous example.

Many sports fans watch highlight shows to keep up-to-speed on games and stories making daily headlines so don't let that get in your way. It's best to jump into the conversation and go from there.

CHAPTER 6

Conversation Exit Strategies

UP TO THIS POINT, we've focused on being able to start a conversation with a sports-loving colleague or client. But how do you make a graceful exit when you feel stumped?

This is the part that tends to scare sports novices the most because they're afraid they won't have all the answers and will end up looking silly. Let me share a little secret with you. I'm a sports broadcaster and an avid sports fan but I don't have all the answers. There will always be something that I don't know or that someone else is more familiar with than me.

Learning to talk sports for business isn't about becoming a know-it-all. The focus should be on the connections and relationships that are created as a result of sports conversations. When you think of it that way, it's not about knowing all the stats and rules; it's about being a good conversationalist and keeping the lines of communication open.

That doesn't mean you'll feel any less panicky when someone asks a question that you don't know the answer to, or when someone asks you to expand on your initial comments about a team that you just started following a couple of weeks ago. These things are bound to happen as you build your sports knowledge base and learn to talk sports. Here are two strategies you can use to shift the momentum of those conversations and help you avoid feeling like you're backed in a corner.

No, but... These two words are not meant to be used as an excuse, but as a qualifying statement that will help you answer without sounding uneasy. Using the word "No" conveys honesty in a situation and the "but" encourages the conversation to continue. Here's an example:

- "Did you see the game last night?"
- "**No, but** what happened?"

Here's another example:

- "Did you see the highlights of that game last night?"
- "**No,** it was Open House at my daughter's school, **but** fill me in. What happened?"

If someone asks you about a game that you didn't watch, the worst thing you could do is lie and say you did. It goes without saying that lying isn't a very effective way to build relationships. But in this situation, if you lie about watching a game and you are asked for more information, you'll be found out quickly by the sports fans in the group and you'll look bad when you have to fess up.

Many novice sports fans or new sports fans place unrealistic expectations on themselves about what it means to be a "real" fan and how many games they should be watching. There is no magic number, and as you've seen throughout the book, many ways exist to follow sports without watching games.

There is no shame in saying you didn't watch a game, or in saying that you didn't see the highlights or that you didn't get a chance to read the sports page. You can still show an interest in the conversation and ask about your colleague's viewpoint.

In fact, in the second example of how to use "No, but" you see how the door to a different conversation is opened. That segues into our second exit strategy.

Define Your Area of Expertise. This is your chance to draw a target around the subject that you feel most comfortable talking about and avoid being subjected to a number of questions that you can't answer or address. Here's an example:

- "Who do you think is going to win the Super Bowl this year?"
- "I'm not much of a football fan, but I like watching basketball."

This strategy works really well in many situations. Here are a couple more examples:

- "I think this year's Red Sox team is going to look a lot like the 2004 team that won the World Series. What do you think?"
- "I moved to Boston about a year ago. That's when I started following the Red Sox, so it's hard for me to make a comparison. I think they'll be fun to watch."

And finally:

- "Hey did you see Seattle might get another basketball team? What do you think the odds of that happening are?"
- "I've seen a couple of headlines in the paper about that, but haven't had a chance to read many of the details."

Each of these examples addresses the conversation topic at hand with honesty and offers a coworker an idea of what follow-up question would resonate. The first example pointed to basketball as a way to keep the conversation going. The second example offered a specific time parameter that could be used in the discussion. Anything that's happened in the last year is fair game, but anything prior to that won't generate much conversation.

The third example addresses the specific concern about getting most of your sports news through sports page headlines, radio up-dates, and the rest of the five-step process in Chapter 3. As you become more comfortable and engage in more sports conversations, chances are you'll be asked for your opinion.

First of all, keep in mind that most sports discussions are opin-ion-based. There's rarely a right and wrong answer except in an argument about a specific stat or outcome. You are entitled to your opinion during a conversation. If you don't feel comfortable sharing, use the approach in the second example as a guide. Be honest about what you know and set parameters about how comfortable you are in talking further.

CHAPTER 7

Make Some Noise

SMALL BUT EFFECTIVE.

It's the way I describe a whistle, particularly the Fox 40 whistle used by football officials everywhere.

I was one of those officials for 10 years. I know firsthand how the sound of that whistle causes a game to come to a screeching halt. The whistle is so loud and clear that it cuts through the noise of a crowded stadium. It is a small and powerful tool.

I will never forget the first time I was handed my whistle and instructed to blow it on the football field. I was a freshman at Southern Methodist University and I was going through intramural flag football training with a handful of other students. We lined up along the edge of the field. One by one we were instructed to blow our whistle. It seemed easy enough, until it was my turn. My first attempt came out as a pitiful dribble of sound. It didn't sound at all like a whistle. I tried again with similar results. I felt my cheeks go red as our instructor chided me on the importance of being able to do this during a game.

As an 18-year-old student it became a make or break moment. And I made it.

The next whistle blast was clean, clear, and loud. I was hooked. That experience propelled me into an officiating career that led to All America honors as a flag football official, a healthy career as a high school official, and credibility in football that I leveraged into a job as the Seahawks sideline radio reporter.

The on-field instructor that night thought I was just timid in front of everyone else, overwhelmed by the situation. He didn't know that I was actually feeling fear.

That whistle is so loud and clear you can't help but catch people's attention. I was afraid of that attention. What happens if someone notices me? What happens if during a game I stop play and everyone listens to me? What happens if all eyes are on me after I blow that whistle?

For those of you thinking, "Of course you're going to get attention for blowing a whistle," I want you to think about this story in the context of sports conversations and the strategies outlined in this book.

I described the whistle as small and effective. The same thing could be said of sports conversations at work.

You've likely heard the phrase "one conversation can change the course of your business forever."

It's true. But it's probably not the conversation that you think.

Often we think of career-changing conversations as the moment when the big contract is signed, or the moment the client you've been courting for months comes on board. Sometimes we think of that career-changing conversation as the one that announces a promotion or raise.

But in every one of those instances, a conversation came long before each of those outcomes. There was a lunch with a potential client, a quick conversation in an elevator, or a first-time meeting at a conference. It's those conversations that we need to pay more attention to, because if those exchanges are awkward, uncomfortable, or unproductive, there's less likelihood of a follow-up conversation.

Conversations are a key tool in relationship-building. The more chances you find to converse with someone, the stronger the relationship. Strong relationships in business increase the likelihood of business transactions and opportunities.

Sports conversations increase those relationship-building opportunities and set you up for future success. When you use sports to communicate with your colleagues, they will notice. They will stop. They will listen. And they will take action.

It's very similar to what happens when you blow a whistle.

There will likely be some fear and some butterflies as you try these techniques. But if you're willing to make some noise, it's worth it.

www.TalkSportytoMe.com